Flat Water

Nebraska Poems

Judy Brackett Crowe

Finishing Line Press
Georgetown, Kentucky

Flat Water
Nebraska Poems

for my family
here and there, now and then

"What you know first stays with you."
Patricia MacLachlan

Nebraska, a name from the mid-1800s meaning "Flat Water," derives from several Native American sources: native Sioux, Omaha-Ponca, and Oto (part of the Siouan family), all of which mean "flat water" and refer to the Platte River, the shallow river that flows through the state. It has long been referred to as being "a mile wide and an inch deep." The first Europeans to see the Platte and to give it its name were French explorers and trappers, who referred to the river as *La Rivière Plate* ("flat river").

ACKNOWLEDGMENTS

These poems first appeared in the following journals:

"Early Birds" *Midwest Prairie Review*
"her hands" *Spillway*
"Flight Plan" *Cultural Weekly*
"Instructions to a New Chicken Farmer" *Midwest Review*
"Marmalade" *The Waterhouse Review*
"Migration" *Canary*
"The Middle of Nowhere" *A Prairie Journal*
"The Other Heaven" *Commonweal*
"Prairie Prom" *Postcard Poems and Prose*
"Swimming Through Summer" *West Marin Review*
"Tomorrow" *Cultural Weekly*
"Where We Came From" *Miramar*
"The Winter's Rocks" *Written Here: The Community of Writers Poetry Review*

I've borrowed the epigraph line from the children's picture book, *What You Know
First,* by Patricia MacLachlan, with engravings by Barry Moser.

I would like to thank the Kimmel Harding Nelson Arts Center in Nebraska City,
Nebraska, for two residency grants, where some of these poems had their beginnings.
Thank you to poets and friends, Molly Fisk, Judie Rae, and Gail Entrekin for their own
good work and for their support and careful reading of my poems. Thanks, also, to
Beth Ford for her help with the manuscript and for the beautiful cover.

Publisher: Leah Maines
Editor: Christen Kincaid
Cover Photo: Judy Brackett Crowe
Author Photo: Sam Crowe
Cover Art & Design: Beth Ford

Printed in the USA on acid-free paper.
Order online: www.finishinglinepress.com

Author inquiries and mail orders:
Finishing Line Press
P. O. Box 1626
Georgetown, Kentucky 40324
U. S. A.

Table of Contents

I. Becoming

II. Migration

Becoming

Geography of a Cloud

Once a long-ago winter's day she drew
a huge map of her world on butcher paper,
using every crayon stub in the small
cedar box that held the bright clear colors
of her life: an immense cloud-shaped world,
endless, with hills and wide rivers,
stick people, kind people like Teacher
and her aunties and her friend Jane,
houses, horses, dogs, sunflowers
and hollyhocks. The torn blue edges
were the sky and whatever lived beyond
the fall-off places and beyond the sky—
roiling deserts, flat black seas, ice-bound
lands—triangle creatures with wiry whiskers
and many legs.

Later, hundreds of thousands of miles later,
bittersweet and periwinkle and Prussian blue
and flesh and magenta later, and thistle, salmon,
gold and silver later, after decades in the fall-off
places, she found herself in that cloud-shaped
map again, the colorful world still smelling
of crayon and cedar, of onions and summer,
and of the fields she'd looked down upon
from her childhood window in that long-ago
time, surprised to find her map so small
and so red, blue, and yellow strange.

A River Runs Under It

Under this flat plain land
great plains grasslands sandhills
middle of nowhere middle of everywhere
though neither truly flat nor truly plain
runs a river

Along hundreds of green-yellow-brown miles
of dales vales and swales
  streams wind
  hills roll
  bluffs rise
and the great shallow Platte
wends its indifferent way
to the Missouri
through cottonwoods
coneflower
goldenrod
milkweed
prairie grass—
  bluestem
  grama
  needle-and-thread

Shocking rocks otherworldly
the shape of horses and ships
tipis and tables pierce the low sky
send their rock roots deep
into the underground river

Creatures of rare and homely
delight call these plains home—
June bug and firefly
fritillary and swallowtail
prairie chicken
bobcat and red fox
eagle and owl
hawk and hare
gray-plumed redheaded Sandhill Crane
gangly graceful part-time Nebraskan

Prairie dog that dog of a squirrel
tunnels deeper these August dog days
Wild ox and wild horse are gone
Creeks vanish streams trickle
The flat river shrinks
its shores puckering

       The girl lies in a meadow
feels the pulse of the river under
wants it to eat its way up cut its way up
   through rock and soil
   through prairie dog tunnels
   through root thickets
wants it to spring forth geyser-like
wants it to pull down the rain

The girl believes this river flows
to other rivers to the sea
around the world and back again
bringing foreign dirt and foreign gifts

Grandmother told her the Pawnee called it
Kicka Kaa'at
waters that live underground

She feels its pull like water in her body
like blood in her veins
She knows it is there as she knows
this place is her home and
that raspberries and lilacs
   need sun
   need water
   need her

3

Blizzard

The snow pebbles stung their faces as the girl and her brother and sister climbed into the buggy that cold, dark, black-and-white morning.

The horse shuffled and snorted, shook her head. Mother's face was red, her hair a cap of snow. *Hush, Frauke,* she said, slapping the mare's flank and waving the children off toward school. Bundled, mittened, and hatted, quilts on their laps, warm bricks under their boots, the children didn't have to hold the reins. Mother always sang, *The horse knows the way.*

Frauke pulled them along the snowy lane, past cottonwood skeletons, drifts like polar bears, like swans, the soft hills all one growing whiteness between the black of the horse and the black of the sky. The girl thought they might be traveling upside down: no sky, no land, no lane.

Teacher hurried them inside and led the horse into the cloak room. *Oh my,* she said. *It's just the four of us today.* The children rubbed Frauke down, she snuffling, her breath warm, wet circles. From the upstairs room, Teacher brought armloads of blankets and pillows, socks, sweaters, dry mittens. She said, *It's the first day of winter. No lessons today!* She read story after story. They danced and marched around the room, sang "Oh, Susannah," "Jingle Bells," "Fly, white butterflies out to sea…." They ate bread and potatoes and apples, cooked in the iron kettle on the Copper-Clad cookstove. Teacher told summer tales: endless sunny days, field-fresh corn, the county fair.

They played "Going Out West," and Verna began: *When I go Out West, I'm taking my best friend Edith.* Glen said, *When I go Out West, I'm taking my best friend Edith…*(pausing and smiling a shy smile), *Verna's best friend Edith…and a bushelful of Grimes Gold apples.* Elna said, *I'm taking Edith, some apples, and Frauke.* Teacher said, *When I go Out West, I'm taking Verna's best friend Edith, a bushelful of Grimes Gold apples, Frauke, and blackberry jam.*

Hours passed, they sang louder, the wind lashed the schoolhouse, snow pinged the windows, branches cracked and thunked on the roof. They fed Frauke oats and carrots. They fed the hungry fires in the Copper-Clad and the potbelly with wood and corncobs, their faces glowing.

Finally, the snow halfway up the windows, a deep quiet fell over them. The lanterns burned out. They sat together on the floor, not knowing whether it was daytime or night. *The first day of winter,* Teacher said again. *The days will grow longer. The men will come when they can. We are safe here. We are always safe among these books, these fires, these songs.* She piled more blankets on and around them and said, *When I go Out West, I'm taking fireflies and hollyhocks.* In one wet-wool-smelling tangle, they drifted to sleep inside the beauty and enormity of that great white silence.

Chimney Fire

If firebells clanged that winter night,
the night the chimney on Peter Bee's
next-door white house caught fire,
if firebells clanged and lights flashed
and fat hoses gushed water,
she does not remember.

In her red woolen coat, its buttons black as beetles,
the child held her mother's sleeve and watched
flame fingers reach out between the bricks.
Icicles dripped from the eaves.
Mother, swaying, humming,
cradled the new baby
swaddled in Grandma's old sweater.
Neighbors half-circled around them,
their breath making clouds.
Peter Bee, fists on hips, looked
not at his chimney but at Old Cat
streaking across ice-crackly grass.
There she goes, he said.

The night wrapped them from
sky to earth, so dark, so bright.
Mother's red-gold cheeks glowed.
The January half-moon hung low,
its shadow side outlined in blue.
Afterwards, they ate pancakes
in some neighbor's warm yellow kitchen.
Walking home, Peter Bee, his hair wild
and silvery, held the girl's hand and said nothing.

Next morning, they found holes in her red coat
and pinprick burns on their faces
and the backs of their hands.
Her mother's soft fingers spread butter
on those spark-made freckles.

She does not remember water
or sirens
or smoke.
She does not remember the fire, exactly.

She does remember that ghost moon
and the sky raining stars and sparks.

That was before the father came back
from the war.
That was before the other children,
before California.
That was before the world opened up,
before the world closed in.
After that night, the world
was never again
so dark or bright.

What the Girl Hears

At first light, she tiptoes past the kitchen window,
breakfast smells of coffee, cinnamon, and sausage drifting
out with the grownups' talk of crops and weather—
corn, oats, alfalfa, drenchers, scorchers, squalls.
In the barn she smiles at the soft moos
and shuffles of the nine Guernseys waiting
to be milked, and at the old sorrel mare's nickering,
eager for her morning walkabout.

Outside in the swing in the dark, the girl hears
the newlyweds walking along the hollyhock row
and whispering something about frogs and warts,
the hollyhocks whispering, too, maybe something
about a lovely girl, a handsome boy.

The visiting grandmother lies next to the girl,
listens to her *Now I lay me down to sleep*
prayers and her *God bless Mama, Daddy, brothers
and sisters, dogs and cats, and cows, chickens,
and horse* prayers, and the grandmother whispers
her own prayers in German and then snores a polite
grandmotherly snore, and the girl wonders
if it is a Germany snore
or a Nebraska snore
or both, jumbled together.

Marmalade

Cotton dress sticking to her sweaty back,
barefoot, nickels in her pocket,
the girl walks to Roy's store for a loaf of bread.

It's still inside, empty,
Roy and Nell in their rooms behind the curtain,
the thick air smelling of coffee.
She likes to walk the side aisle
where the jams and jellies live,
dressed in their red and purple berry labels.
There's also lemon curd, lime marmalade.
She's never tasted limes.

She plucks a jar off the shelf and hears
noises from the back—a stranger's voice,
scuffling, harsh whispers, whimpers.
Somehow she knows to crouch
and fold herself, to freeze.
Clutching the marmalade, fearing
the dusty lid might make her sneeze,
she holds her breath and listens
to the clink and rustle
of money, rough talk,
Roy and Nell afraid.

Bootsteps shake the floor, the screendoor slams.
She waits, she waits, then breathes again
and stands and peeks around the corner.
The screen frames a man's back—
a farmer's cap, overalls straps.
He disappears and the screen is blank—
wire squares, sunlight.

She hears Roy's voice on the telephone,
wipes the dust from the lid on her damp dress,
carefully sets the jar on the shelf, and slides
out the door into the white-hot day.
Licking her dusty fingers,
the girl walks toward home,
her mouth dreaming of limes.

Cousins and Indians

This winter Sunday afternoon, our house is packed
with relatives—loud-talking uncles, red-apple-cheeked aunts.
Nickerson Bahners, Big Island Pascoes, Wyoming Leshers.
Wyoming!
The women sip coffee;
the men drink beer, play cards,
smoke cigarettes (Uncle Al, a cigar).
We kids tear through the house, chasing and hollering
till Aunt Mid calls out, "Wild Indians! Go sit
for awhile." But she's wearing a smile
and everyone's happy.
Our house is alive.

Tall Uncle Mike and my dad herd us
into the Pontiac—two kids in front, seven in back,
pushing, poking, laughing, and we drive
through gray slushy streets to the movies downtown.
We've each got a quarter and a brown bag of popcorn.
The babies and grownups stay home.

Slipping into the dark we sink into our seats,
filling a row—
Terry and Susan; Darrel and Janice;
Keith, Buddy, and Wayne;
my brother Lanny and me.
It's Lanny's first movie; he sits on his knees
in the seat next to mine.
There's a funny cartoon—birds and mice
and a cat on fire. The music grows loud
and the movie begins. Standing in stirrups,
a cowboy on horseback on a clifftop
looks out over a valley and points
to the Indians gathering and bellowing below.

Lanny asks, "Is this real?" Keith says, "Yep,
we've got Indians in Wyoming. Be still."

When the chief waves his feather staff
and whoops his war cry, Lanny crowds into my seat.
I pinch him, he hollers. I tell him I'll give him the bird skull

and feathers I've hidden under the porch if he'll
just
be
quiet.
When it's over, bright lights,
Lanny's asleep, his bird-mouth wide open.
I pinch him, not hard.

We go home to potato-soup supper, and
we're eating and talking when Mom looks around.
"Where's Lanny?"
Uncle Mike shouts,"Jeepers!" and we run to the car,
Uncle Mike, my dad, and me.
It's dark now, a few snowflakes falling,
the streets crunchy not slushy.

He's standing on the curb in his blue sweater,
in the creamy light under a streetlight moon,
hands in his pockets, looking lost.
We wave and kind of laugh as Dad speeds up
and drives to the corner,
past the movie house,
past Lanny, my brother.
Through the back window, I watch him run
to catch up, all wobbly, hands still in his pockets.
He slides onto my lap and gives me a grin,
but there are tears on his cheeks.
I pinch him,
not hard.

Later, in bed, baby sisters asleep in their crib,
he pulls my hair and wakes me.
He says, "Jude, I was scared."
He says, "Jude, did all those wild Indians die?
Were they bad?"

Becoming

Growing toward their grown-up selves,
three cousins graduated from bailing
out of the swing to dangling
from the rope & dropping
into the creek to climbing
to the top of the grain bins & jumping
into the scratchy oats,
knee deep, hip deep, to diving,
arms flapping like crazy,
from the wash-house roof, landing
& rolling in the loamy clover patch—
daring one another to higher
& farther jumps.

Toward the end of summer, their derring-do
turned to the crafting of wings—gauntlet wings
of beeswax, cornstalks, poultry feathers,
twine & thin wire filched from the tool cupboard—
& plotting takeoffs from the cooptop,
the treehouse, the housetop, the barntop,
the high, steep roof of the church,
& thrashing around the yard, loving
the swishing, whistling wing sounds.

For their maiden flight, from the third-floor
sleeping porch, they lined up on the sill,
chirping, crowing, whooping, squawking—
"I'm a red-tailed hawk!"
"'I'm a raven!"
"I'm a pterodactyl!"
"I'm a golden eagle!"
"I'm a sandhill crane!"
The littlest one cried,
"I'm a…I'm a barn swallow!"
Running out of birds,
they took deep breaths,
touched wings,
& flew.

Early Birds

Up before dawn, just like the farmers, my uncle Earl
says, and helps me into the sidecar of the silver
Indian Chief motorcycle (*Did a real Indian make this?*

Earl says, *You bet!*). I'm crammed in between baseball
stuff and newspapers—*Omaha World Herald, Fremont Guide
and Tribune*—mittened and under a blanket in winter,

or barefoot and a little chilly in the warming summer
air. My uncle Earl is a teenager; I'm seven, eight.
Sometimes he brings cinnamon rolls.

I hand him a paper, he folds it, tucks it
into a perfect square, throws it, and it lands
on the porch every time (baseball practice),

the only sounds some chirpy birds, the putt-putting
of the Indian, papers rustling, a clunk as each one
finds the strike zone. Sometimes Slowpoke, the big

black-and-brown dog, follows us for a block or two and bites
at the tires. Earl always tries to beat the sun; we always do,
the sky turning cotton-candy pink as we finish.

He drops me at home, and I go back to bed to catch
a few winks before breakfast or read a chapter
in one of the books piled next to me and wait

for the rest of the world to wake up and discover
what's happened in their sleep—our gift to them
with their coffee, their eggs and bacon and toast,

our newspapers spread out and shared across
quiet tables all over town.

Potato by Moonlight

Sweets for the sweet, the grandfather says, handing
the girl a carrot, still dirt-warm and dirt-damp,
as they walk along the rows of potato hills,
eating carrots, pulling off potato bugs,
filling a dusty feed sack
(Ogallala Quality Rosebud Flour)
with the odd-looking, wriggling insects.

In the evenings, she sits with her grandmother
in the porch swing, snapping peas, eating a few,
humming along with the peas pinging
in the blue-speckled tin bowl, the swing creaking,
the crickets cricketing, the grandmother talking
about blizzards and babies, a tea towel
piled with radishes and a hillock of salt between them.

The girl tosses radish tops and pea pods into the potato-
bug bag, shakes it, and weaves through the last fireflies
across the lawn to the waiting, scolding chickens.
On her way back, she detours through the garden,
pulls up a potato, pauses at the spigot
to rinse off the dirt, and eats it in the moonlight,
thinking that there is something of the moon
in the taste of these vegetables...
and something of sadness, too.

Swimming Through Summer

We set out to swim through the fields
toward the ends of the Earth,
trying to walk partway on our hands
as our father liked to do—
        pennies, nickels, dimes,
        cellophane-wrapped mints raining
        from his pockets, his pantlegs ruffling
        up to his knees—
and hours later we would wade our way home
to the long evenings, and he would try to teach us how—
        something like a frog squat,
        palms spread on the grass,
        knees propped on our elbows,
        legs slowly reaching for sky,
        and we'd teeter there a few dizzy moments
then float through the twilight to supper, coins
jingling in our pockets, mints and clover
on our tongues, lightning-bug smears on our foreheads,
our heads damp-cloudy with downside-up wonders.

Pony Girl

Never a pony on the porch on Christmas morning or on her birthday. Just
a palm-slapping-hip gallop down the mean streets across the tracks, the early
Burlington just past, on its track-tethered way to the mountains, the far valleys.

Pony girl circles the outskirts of town, swishing through tall grasses
and milkweed, past corrals, pastures, fields, past hemmed-in horses and sad-eyed
cows to the turnaround tree, wondering if one day she'll not turn around,

if she'll follow the Burlington echo, cantering west toward the far valleys,
toward the setting sun, her green eyes shining, milkweed floss in her mane.

Flight Plan

Bone blades jut where her wings once grew.
Rolling her shoulders back and down,
she can feel the pulse, the strength of them,
can almost remember flying.

Riding the bike down the steep and winding
pot-holed lane—airborne, almost. Swinging
on the old saddle hanging from the rafters
in the hayloft, hay bales stacked

against the walls, mice nests, bird nests, barn
cats prowling, the owl tucked into his high-up
corner, haydust motes fogging the air,
she sneezing and swinging—no horse,

just girl and saddle, the loft door thrown
open to the green world, she wondering
if she can swing high enough, fast enough,
far enough, swim/fly out the door and dive

into the pond or the house-high haystack.
No, not the haystack—needles, errant pitchforks.

How to Make Ice Cream

Be a child in a middle place, a place of north/south, east/west
go-on-forever roads   Think about one day going on forever
west or south on one of them   Think nothing of snowdrifts
taller than you or flooded pastures, floating cows, thin milk
that tastes like grass   In the summer, stay with relatives who
work the farm from dawn to dark, who let you be you, not
deciding to or thinking about it, just allowing   One early July
morning, perhaps the best day ever, gather windfall late peaches
just the southwest side of ripe, wash and peel and mash them

That afternoon, after church, the aproned aunts, uncles in their
Sunday clothes, a couple of grandmas and grandpas, your mom and dad,
brothers and sisters, a passel of cousins and dogs, and the usual flies
have gathered   Bedsheets drape the hilly tables on the side yard—
potato, Jell-O, 3-bean salads; fried chicken; buttermilk biscuits;
and more underneath

Uncle prepares the old bucket (tin) in another bucket (wood staves),
dasher and crank, chipping ice from a block the size of a boot while
Aunt simmers this morning's milk (bluish, cream-topped) with egg
yolks, sugar, vanilla, and stirs in your peaches   The kids take turns
churning until the crank says *No More*, and Uncle pulls out the dasher,
packs down the iced cream, and covers it with more ice and a blanket
for later   The churners' reward—licking the dasher, thick
with sweet snow   The barn cats catch drips

The long afternoon wanes—food, talk, tag and croquet, grownups lolling
on quilts on the grass   Finally, a few songs, peaches and ice cream

Now, notice the fireflies, the meadow smell in the air, the cars chugging
away down the south lane, hands waving out windows, toward Monday
and work, toward forever

Tomorrow

This flat wide-open place is
airless, but she doesn't know that
yet. She dreams, walks to
the library, checks out
her five-books-per-day ration,
sits under
a poplar on
the way home and reads a couple,
reads the rest that night, treks back to
the library tomorrow,
thinking that her bare feet are carving ruts in
the earth. Running to
the edge of
town she wonders at
the line at
the curb of
the world where green or brown or white meets
blue—the beginning or the end?
The orderly fields—
in summer
blindingly green and smelling of
dirt and sun rays,
in winter
crop-stubbled or snow-buried—
are alluring and terrifying, pulling her to
their plainness, their silences.
She writes songs and sings them to
herself, to
the books, to
the fields, to
the sky.
She dreams. She waits for
something.
She leaves.

Migration

Nebraska

Oh, yes, it's flat, mostly—plains, prairie,
laconic landscape, windswept midwestern
everything. The heartland, flatter than a pancake.
The Nebraska Line, the jokey name
for when the heart monitor shows a line
like the east-west roads across the plains.

Except…notice the rolling hills, the buttes,
the bluffs along the rivers—the Missouri, the Platte,
the North Loup, the Niobrara, the Dismal.
From the tops of the bluffs you can see—plaid fields;
the blackest dirt in springtime, furrowed and waiting
for green; prairie grasses tall enough to hide in,
to get lost in; and strange rock outcrops
—volcanic ash, clay, sandstone—a horse,
a table, a chimney. The settlers, passers-through,
from forest lands and higher hills, were curious about,
even frightened by these rugged soaring monoliths.

Macsen thought if he climbed the tallest rock
he could see the parentheses of seas
on left and right, the seas he knew he'd get to see
one day. His sister Carys said he'd see
only more prairie—Iowa, maybe the Dakotas,
Wyoming, Missouri—maybe buffalo. And so
he never climbed; he never saw the sea.
Instead, he swam in tallgrass prairies
—Indiangrass, big bluestem, switchgrass—
deep enough to drown in.

the platte

you cannot step into the same river twice they say   not true i am the same river
always was always will be stretching from colorado to missouri   not really
stretching from & to but joining up with being part of

                                          not many know my
underself the great river part beneath   plains indians called it *kicka kaa'at*
   platte is not a grand name not my real name anyway   if you could even begin
to know my name you would first taste me live in me listen to me through every
season for years & years   the ice the warming the rocks rising bluffs forming
wind shaping & smoothing shrinking spreading changing

                                        you might call me
"the river that is part of all that ever was & ever will be   river that slakes thirst
that cleanses that gives life to this land this world without end *amen shanti
silua you bet*"   here from the beginning from the before anything & anyone

i have seen not seen exactly but held embraced meandered through this lush
& beautiful life-giving   life-holding   life-taking land   braiding rebraiding
my channels my streams my trickles   i have known the moving & growing
creatures the rooted things   such abundance in me near me above & below

        earth-tied ones—cottonwood willow graceful prairie grasses
        birds of clever design—waterfowl raptors singers
        four-footeds—prairie dog buffalo horse
        two-footeds—the first ones & later indians another unsuitable
                name   they might be called "those who came after long after
                long long after the first ones"   they gave themselves other
                names family names—sauk oglala oto ponca pawnee
        then more two-footeds—strangers settlers with wagons & cattle
            tools & fences

i have taken them into my watery self & into my colors   earthbrown grassgreen
skyblue   so here i am & have been not deep not fast but steady & alive between
earth's depths & sky   wind rain snow tears & sweat become me move in me
through me out of me   & i remember   i know it all hold it all give it all back

dip your fingers into this river & remember with me

Migration: The Gathering

       In the cold twilight, sandhill cranes gather in cornfields along the river,
the beautiful, the beautiful river, countless flocks of ten or twenty or more,
gleaning snacks from crop stubble before lifting off and settling on sandbars
in the frigid waters of the Platte.
       On the icy bridge a hundred yards away, seven
silent watchers gather, their noses burning and dripping, fingers numbing,
and set up tripods and fancy cameras (no flashes allowed) while the cranes
fidget, making gargly, warbly noises, elbowing one another, checking
on their mates and their spindly-legged young—colts, they're called—
watching the watchers, and finally quieting as the March darkness deepens,
enveloping the thousands of cranes, now one inky, shifting mass
in the shallow depths.
       Before first light the watchers return to spy
as the cranes awaken and shuffle about until the sky is right and they rise
from their marshy roost in a cloud, one whooshing ululation like angels
on their way to some kind of crane heaven or just to cruise to nearby fields
to feed another day or few, and then in great herds, like upside-down cyclones,
soar to the thermals, gliding and riding them north, miles and miles
of sun-frosted ribbons.
       If sandhills had four legs, they'd be horses, Pegasi.
Their lightning—silver shooting through blue, their thunder—echoes of nine
million years of wingbeat and song across the plains.
       Earthbound, the watchers
are left to wait another year, admiring their beautiful, flat photographs. And
the shallow Platte abides, still and shining.

The Nickerson Store

Next to the counter, a red cooler squats,
pop bottles floating in ice water, ice squares
as big as piglets, water so cold it burns
your fingers. Dry goods and mustard
and weevily flour and vanilla and Ivory soap
(*It Floats!*) wait on newspaper-lined shelves.

Up the stairs on Wednesday nights,
a farm wife reads scripture,
a few women sing, their darning
and babies in their generous laps.

Down the dusty street, cowboy music
drifts out the tavern door. Inside: boot
tracks on the sawdusty floor; a pool
table; lean brown men in farmer caps,
leaning, talking, drinking;
smells of beer and hay.

Under a waning old moon, few stars, rough
clouds, a woman paces the street
through hymns and cowboy songs,
past the shuttered store, past the Pontiac
with three sleeping children folded
into each other on the back seat,
sticky pop bottles on the floor.

Now, one of the children is gone,
the men are gone, the woman, gone.
Tavern and store are gone. Sagging
curtains blur the upstairs windows,
anonymous dim light seeps into the night,
ghosting the street, and a lone dusty car waits,
missing two wheels, listing to starboard.

Milking Time

These dozen are Nebraska cows, black-and-white
Holsteins, cousins surely of Billy Collins' Irish cows,
resting on the "black-and-white maps of their sides."
(You'll never again look at a Holstein without
thinking: *There's the Platte River...There's Aurora...
There's York...There's the North Loup.*
Or maybe it's Tasmania or the wild Irish west coast.)

In the far fields, ringed with butterfly weed and winecup,
the cows are just now rising from their open-eyed
siestas, heaving themselves up—front legs, back legs—
and forming their raggedy line,
noses following
swinging tails,
udders full and swaying,
plodding along
the meandering path
to the paddock,
to the barn,
each one nodding
into her familiar stanchion,
facing her sister in the next aisle
and giving her a soft
"Hello again" moo.

The farmer perches on his one-legged stool
next to each girl in turn (he calls them girls),
leans his forehead into her warm side, and croons—
"Hey, Bossie...Hey, Sally...Hey, Mrs. B...
Hey, Lizzie Jones." The girls munch fresh hay,
a half dozen yowling barn cats wait
for a squirt of warm blue grassy milk...

and a fifth of the globe away,
some Irish farmer does the same—
"Ay, Fiona...Ay, Ailish...
Ay, Nora...Ay, Missy O'Byrne."

Instructions to a New Chicken Farmer

Come springtime, buy a few chicks from Miss Aggie,
settle them in the brooder, move them to the new coop
when they get feisty, let them run about the fenced pasture
to forage for worms and bugs, give them table scraps
and organic feed. Watch them peck and prance
and scuffle in the yard. Watch them grow.

All summer long, think of family picnics under the elms,
twilight, pink-sky suppers on the side porch,
and think of chicken—
        rosemary-rubbed and roasted
            grilled veggies
            warm peppery biscuits
        batter-dipped and fried, crispy skin
            potato salad
            home-canned pickles
        marinated in lime, cilantro, and orange zest
            homemade tortillas
            salsa fresca
and always your tender side-yard lettuce
drizzled with milk and sugar and cider vinegar.

Every evening, cast handfuls of corn
from your apron pockets to your little flock.
Do not give them names. Give them
fresh water, fresh straw in their cubbies.
Praise their shiny coats, their bright eyes. Listen
to the music of their gurgles, clucks, and wing flaps.
Gather their brown eggs, admire the marigold yolks,
the star-bright whites.

When it's time, sharpen the hatchet.
Choose the first one. Lead her to the cottonwood stump.
She will look you in the eye and lay her head down.
You'll set aside the hatchet, and sigh,
Hello, Genevieve.

Goodbye

Prairie Prom

What if some prairie chickens and sandhill cranes and maybe a whooper or two threw a party when no one was looking, not even the photographers in camouflage hunkered down in their branch-roofed blinds with their long lenses, their granola bars and thermos bottles. And what if the birds invited some spoonbills and ibises, though the dance field might be a bit frosty for those warm bloods. Picture conga line, bunny hop: cranes preening and prancing, stocky chickens chortling, scurrying about, stamping their feet, weaving in and out through dozens of twiggy legs.

Prairie Doo-wop and Prairie Motown, rock 'n' roll, the twist. Yodels and whoops. Eyes locking, eyes glancing away. Shaking and clacking their pointy beaks, their curly beaks, their flat beaks. A few shy ones huddling on the sidelines: wings tucked, watching, longing. Can't you just see the slow dances, The Penguins crooning: "Earth angel, earth angel, will you be mi..ine, my darling dear…" Dancers' breath cloudlets. Wings lifting and drifting, wingtips touching. Red, white, and gray feathers swirling in the downy moonlight.

Those Who Know Best

The great-grandmother feels sorry for the sheep,
the cows, even the pigs,
sorry for their blind little lives,
for the way they're pushed from here to there
and back again,
but not sorry for the chickens—
their brave take-no-prisoners strutting about,
their sassy talk.
She wishes she could be like the chickens,
thinks she once was like that, but has been
for so long at the mercy of time, of the weather,
of those who know best (who think they know best).
On good days she chases the pesky rooster
around the yard, just to feel that energy, that fluster.
She scoops a couple of leghorns onto her aproned lap,
strokes their warm feathers, clucks back to them,
divvies up blue corn.
Sentient beings, she thinks. *Sisters.*

The Winter's Rocks

On a sunny-cold spring afternoon, the earth still frozen,
he harvests the winter's bounty of rocks, bucketsful,
and muses, as he does every year—*What a crop,*
too bad they're not edible. A saver of string-too-
short-to-be-saved, he uses everything his land

gives up, curses or gifts—burdock and chickweed,
garlic and onions, potatoes and peas. As the sun falls
behind the far hills, he straightens and drifts across
his field to the old graveyard, to the time-and-
weather-smoothed and sunken stones, some

with faint angels and lambs etched in pink granite,
none more recent than a hundred years ago. He always
visits the old man lying between two wives—
Interesting rumbles down there, he thinks—
and spots a patch of wild mustard sprouting between

a lamb and an angel, plucks a pocketful, and goes
back to sort the rocks and fill the ruts in the lane,
to make stone soup for one for supper.

her hands

folded now
no longer
working peeling pushing
twisting scraping pounding
stitching planting picking
patting smoothing soothing

thumbs twiddle rhythmically
now fast now slow
north to south
south to north
then pause

her gaze threaded
to her pensive restive hands
set at some long-ago mist place

she'll blink and blink and say
chickens are the prettiest things
or *roast is ready   where is he*
or *storm's comin' on   oh yes*

The Other Heaven

On nights with little moon or none,
the near-blind great-grandmother settles
in her chair in the middle of the orchard,
bare branches or new leaves or hard-green
or just-right or too-late pears
around her, depending,

and listens to the music of the spheres. She makes
a circle, a kind of moon, with thumbs and pointers
touching, and looks up through it to where the sisters
or the queen or the swan might be and waits
for the music to begin—whistling or humming
or bluesy harmonica or plaintive fiddle, sometimes
(she smiles at this) a harp,

and all of it, lullaby or symphony, faint and strange.
Oftentimes, she stirs to find the night sky gone
and rises to the crackle of the sun waking up the pears.

The Things We Saved & Left Behind

Round things—bottle caps (beer, root beer, Nehi grape & orange pop) with cork
liners you could pop out, put the caps outside your t-shirt, press corks inside
—viola!—a dandy piece of jewelry (we always said viola, even though we knew
it was voilà…waLA!)

> marbles— aggies, cat's eyes, puries, bumblebees

> tin foil—peeled from gum wrappers & cigarette packages collected
> from street gutters (polio water!) & rolled into silver globes

> zinc pennies, birthday silver dollars

> lumpy balls of pieces of string too short to be saved

> piles of snowballs

Big Chief tablets with brownish, wood-splintery, turquoise-dotted, lined pages
   filled with penciled numbers from 1 to millions
   filled with funny stories "What the Dog Brought Home"—newspapers; slabs
      of butter (we ate the butter, left on some neighbor's porch pre-dawn
      by the milkman; never knew whose porch); golf balls, tennis balls,
      sticks & rocks; one corduroy jacket (the father wore it for years)
   filled with words, always words, from books, from the grownups—
      "son of a seacook," "Don't stand there looking like a tree full of owls,"
      "Jesus, Mary, Joseph, & Fred!," "Don't make me come back there!,"
      honyock, viola!, eureka!, prairie, cottonwood, hummingbird,
      Kicka Kaa'at, auf Wiedersehen

Baby teeth the fairy rejected or forgot, bird nests, Cracker Jack toys, tin whistles,
feathers

Waves—We stood on the curb in front of Grandma's, waving at cars, counting
the waves back at us; Old Mrs. Kroeber never waved, told our grandma
we were honyocks.

We arranged & rearranged all those treasures on windowsills & bookshelves,
then abandoned them when our house was sold, when we auctioned off our lives
& left, waving *auf Wiedersehen* to the prairie, to the cottonwoods,
to the grandma.

The Middle of Nowhere

Through the prairie grasses
tall and thick and wet-green
beyond the town beyond the fences
I walk along the wagon ruts.
In the middle
          of nowhere
I come upon a tomato plant.
              A tomato plant!
There's no farm here no house
no aproned farmer's wife
to tie it to a stake with string
saved from the butcher's neat package.

I wonder at this volunteer
yellow spiky blossoms
7 pea-size pea-green tomatoes
(Big Boy? Early Girl?)
and ask it plain:
          Who planted you
          and why and when?

Perhaps a hiker a wanderer like me
dropped seeds unknowingly
or mischievous dug a hole
and put you here.

I pull a leaf inhale that strong wet rough
smell that smells like nothing else on Earth,
and here's my answer:
through this fragrant fog
across the waves of grass
in the shade of cottonwoods
I see a prairie schooner
from Maine perhaps or Carolina
with pots and pans and quilts and hopes.

They rest a day or two
cook and mend and sleep and sleep
slip naked into the creek
sigh and set out once again

but leave behind tomato seeds
to hibernate for six score years
until rain and chance and sun
and movement of the earth
in this place at this time
decide.

I pick one tiny fruit for proof of this
and stroll along.
Late in summer home again
I'll smile to know the secret of
half a dozen fat red juicy
sun-filled tomatoes
        in the middle of nowhere
        in the middle of everything
        that matters.

I'll wonder what I've left behind of me.

Where She Is

She slips out the door
feels Auntie watching
            at the kitchen window
skips round the third bend
crosses the double tracks
pausing to press an ear to the rail
            metal-ly hum
            tangy smell of iron

The important thing—no one
knows where she's going

She doubles back, sidles through
            a break in the windbreak trees
crouch-slinks through tall grasses
hears grasshopper chirps
            magpies *mag-mag-mag*-ing
            something swishing low to the ground
smells dusty sun rays
sucks on a spear of grass
finds her teepee in the alder roots
            near Swift Fox Creek
tinkers with her treasures
            stick matches from the tin above the stove
            Auntie's earring, just one
            hard candies in waxed paper twists
            rose hips

Years later, the important thing—no one
knows where she is

She parks the rental car down the lane
walks toward town a ways
rounds the third bend
crosses the double tracks
lays her ear on the rail
            no hum today

doubles back
wades through grasses
            & wild rose brambles

hears grasshopper chirps
        magpies
        crackles
        rustles & trills
Swift Fox Creek a trickle
three-toed prints along the
        crackled clay banks
What's there?
Nothing
not even the alder

Where We Came From

If there isn't a special day named "Go Back
Where You Came From Even If You Were Never
There," there should be, and I will take you
to that middle place, take some of what's left

of you, wrapped in the funny papers, tucked
into a picnic basket, along with bologna sandwiches
(white bread, no mayo, no mustard), a cold Dr Pepper,
salted peanuts, and a chocolate cake. I will sit

under a cottonwood on the frame of a rusty tractor,
eat the food you used to love, and think of the day
we brought our mother's ashes here, to these fields where
she drove the tractor with her father riding the combine

behind her in the August dust and heat, a rope around
his wrist, the other end tied to her arm, that he could pull
if the hook slipped or if something else went haywire.
Our grandfather once spent half a day (or a whole day,

or three or four days) up in this same tree (or some other tree)
when Bell Crick flooded and waited for the firemen
to row down to save him. We were not there then,
we were not anywhere then, but we might as well

have been, the story in our heads forever.
On this day I will leave you here with them.
The fall fields are stubble,
littered with dried corn,
gold kernels hard as rocks
and bright as memory.

remembering is what

sandhill cranes do,
have done—
thousands millions flying
from cold north
through middlemost latitudes
southward & back again
for millennia

is what
western monarchs do—
their autumn-colored rabble winging
to eucalyptus groves
to a kind of hanging-in-air
hibernation
some inner lodestar telling them
where & when

is what
the river does or tries to do—
eddies crags vortexes
& dams be damned

is what I want to do—
remember my way from & to
necessary latitudes longitudes
outer & inner landscapes
not sure-winged like sandhill or monarch
but meandering
sashaying
remembering
like the river